Tracing Letters
for Preschoolers

by Preschool Kidlix

A  LIKE .....

COLOR ALL OBJECTS THAT BEGIN WITH THE LETTER A

APPLE

B LIKE .....

COLOR ALL OBJECTS THAT BEGIN WITH THE LETTER B

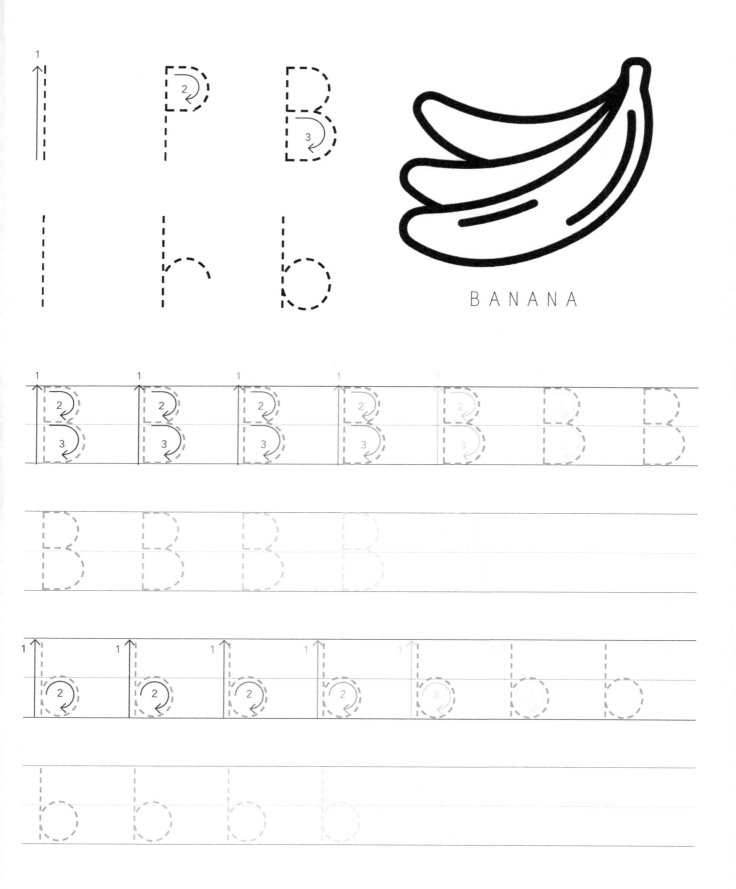

BANANA

BBBBBBBBBBBB

BBBBBBBBBBB

BBBBBBBBBBBB

BBBBBBBBBBB

BBBBB

b b b b b b b b b b b b

b b b b b b b b b b b b

b b b b b b b b b b b b

b b b b b b b b b b b b

b b b b b b b b b b b b

C

LIKE .....

COLOR ALL OBJECTS THAT BEGIN WITH THE LETTER C

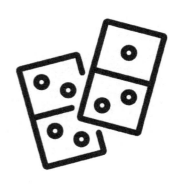
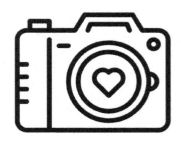

CLOWN

D

LIKE .....

COLOR ALL OBJECTS THAT BEGIN WITH THE LETTER D

DUCK

DDDDDDDDDD

DDDDDDDDDD

DDDDDDDDDD

DDDDDDDDDD

E

LIKE .....

COLOR ALL OBJECTS THAT BEGIN WITH THE LETTER E

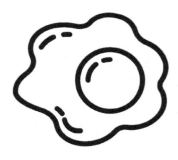

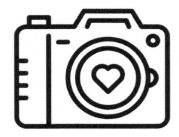

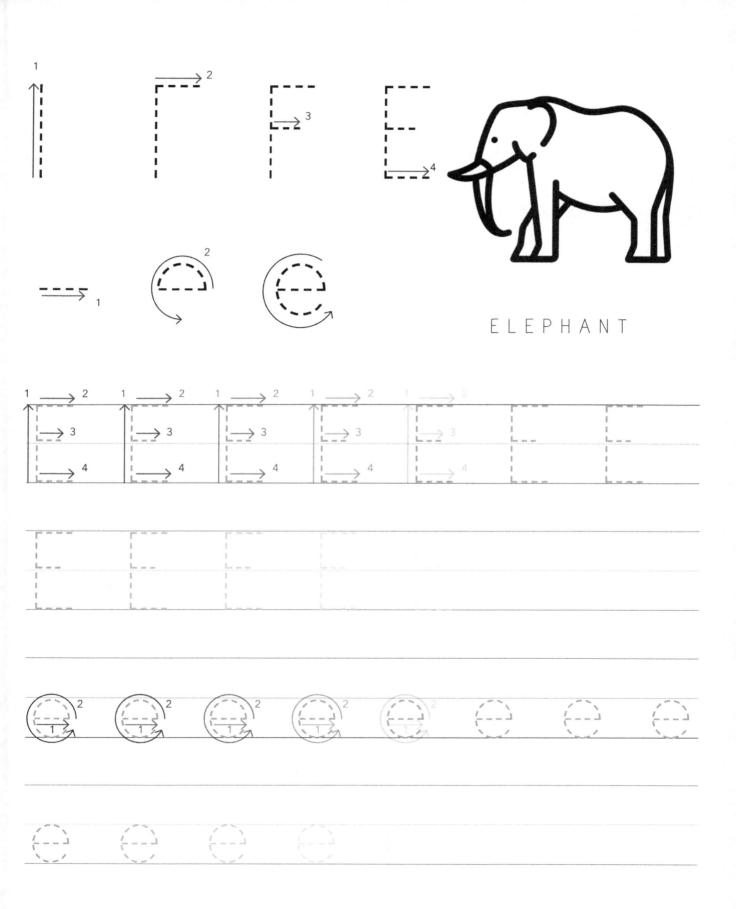

ELEPHANT

F

LIKE .....

COLOR ALL OBJECTS THAT BEGIN WITH THE LETTER F

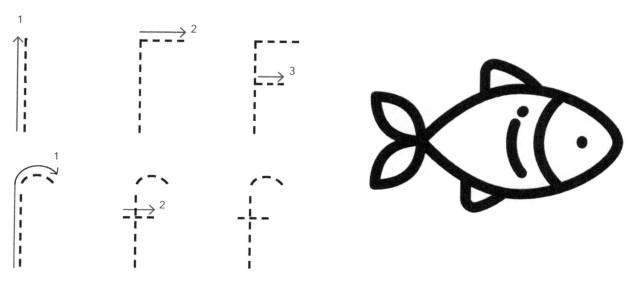

F I S H

G
LIKE .....

COLOR ALL OBJECTS THAT BEGIN WITH THE LETTER G

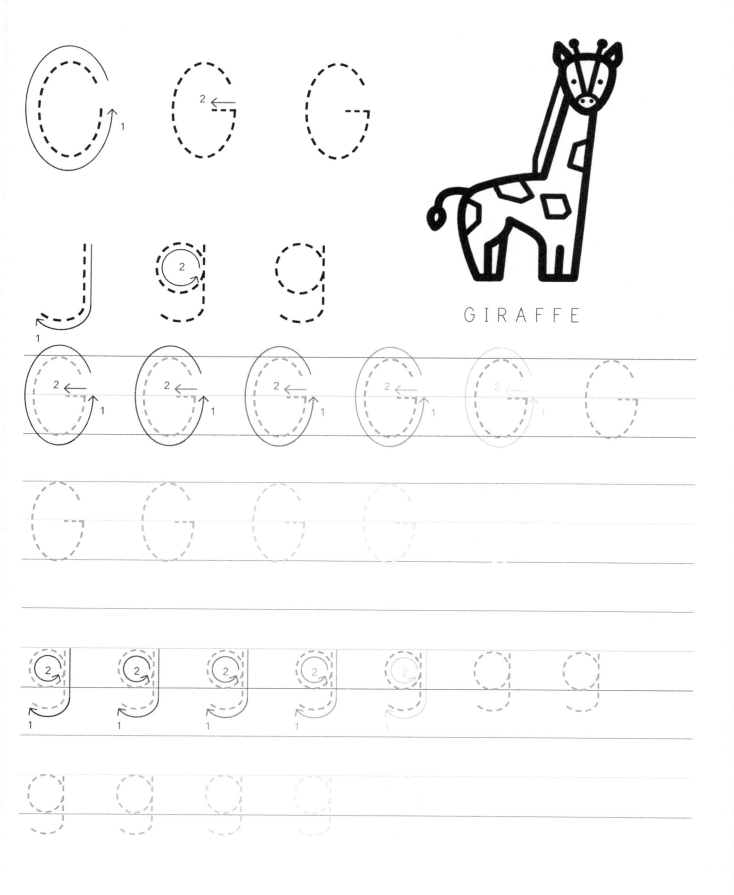

GIRAFFE

H LIKE .....

COLOR ALL OBJECTS THAT BEGIN WITH THE LETTER H

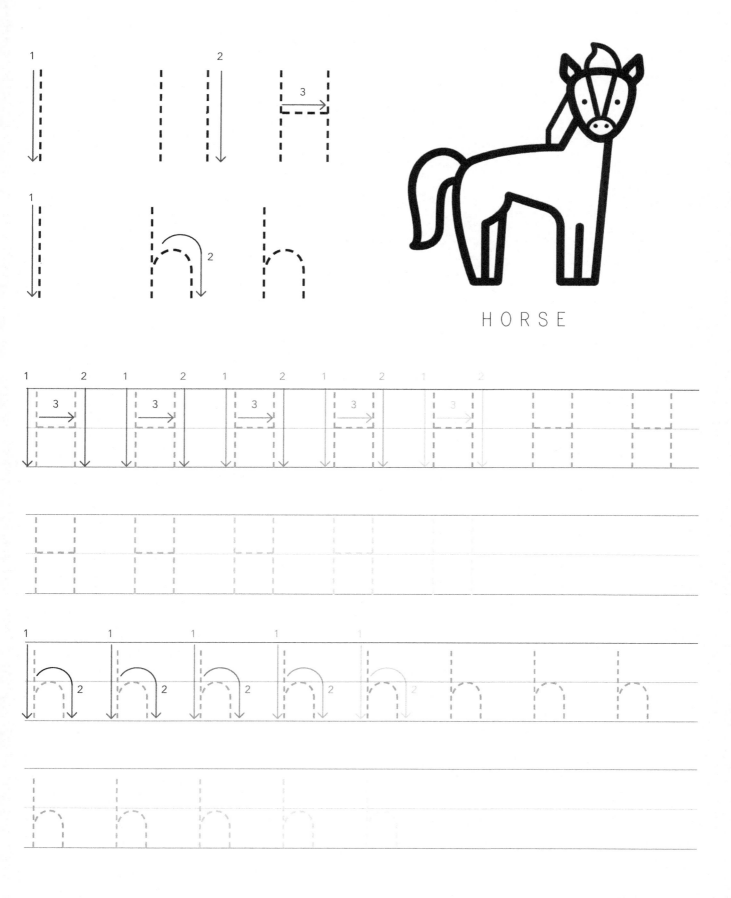

HORSE

I

LIKE .....

COLOR ALL OBJECTS THAT BEGIN WITH THE LETTER I

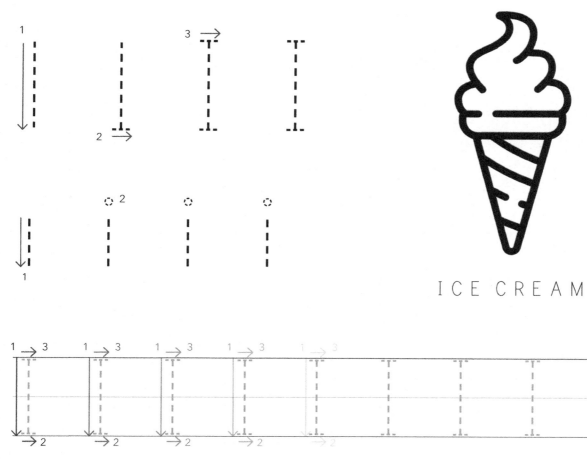

ICE CREAM

J

LIKE .....

COLOR ALL OBJECTS THAT BEGIN WITH THE LETTER J

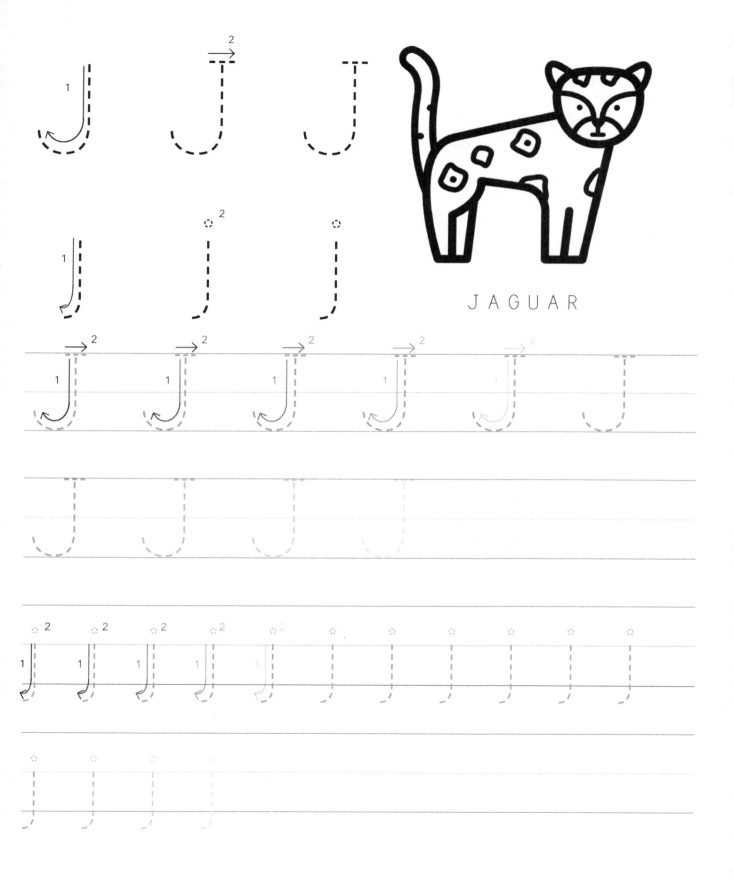

JAGUAR

K LIKE .....

COLOR ALL OBJECTS THAT BEGIN WITH THE LETTER K

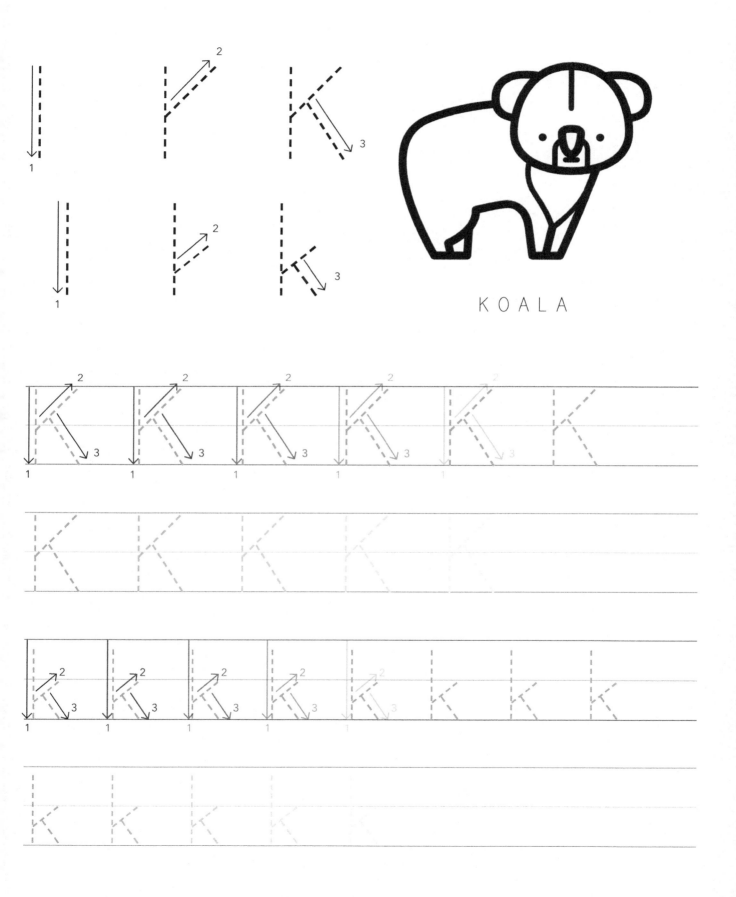

KOALA

L

LIKE .....

COLOR ALL OBJECTS THAT BEGIN WITH THE LETTER L

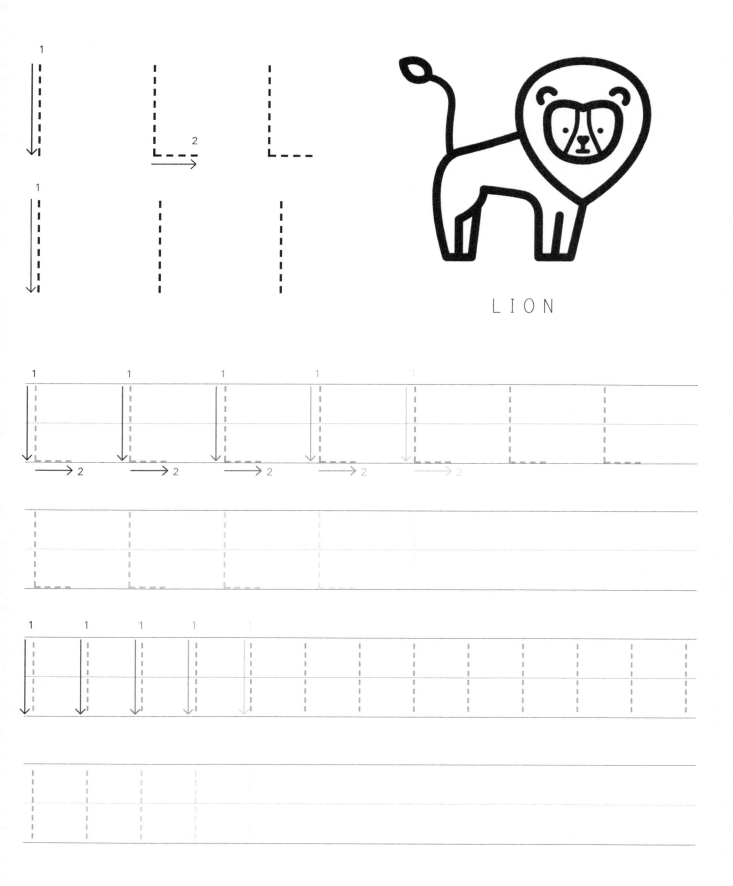

LION

M

LIKE .....

COLOR ALL OBJECTS THAT BEGIN WITH THE LETTER M

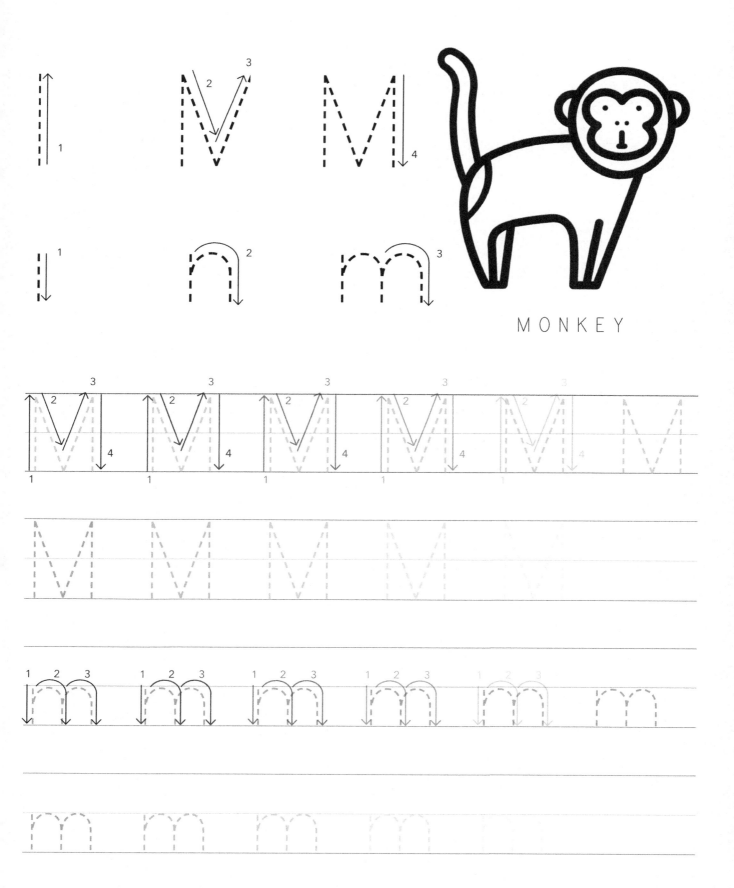

MONKEY

N

LIKE .....

COLOR ALL OBJECTS THAT BEGIN WITH THE LETTER N

NOSE

O

LIKE .....

COLOR ALL OBJECTS THAT BEGIN WITH THE LETTER O

OCTOPUS

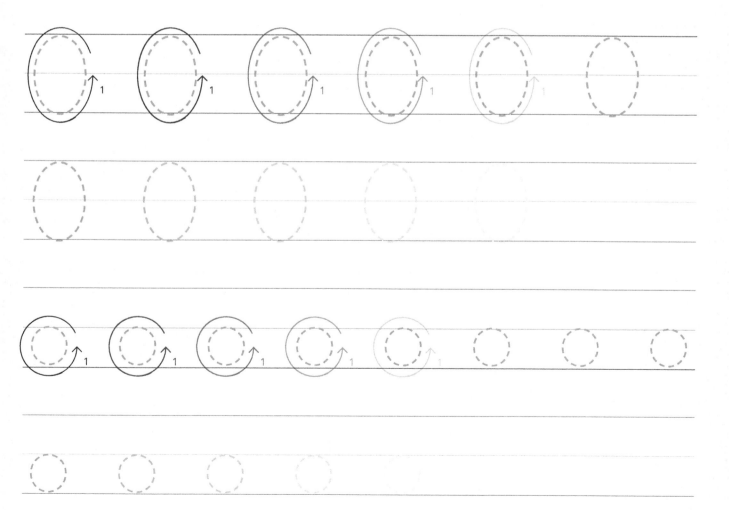

P

LIKE .....

COLOR ALL OBJECTS THAT BEGIN WITH THE LETTER P

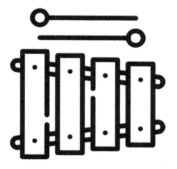

PENGUIN

P P P P P P P P P P

P P P P P P P P P P

P P P P P P P P P P

P P P P P P P P P P

p p p p p p p p p p p p

p p p p p p p p p p p p

p p p p p p p p p p p p

p p p p p p p p p p p p

p p p p p p p p p p p p

Q

LIKE .....

COLOR ALL OBJECTS THAT BEGIN WITH THE LETTER Q

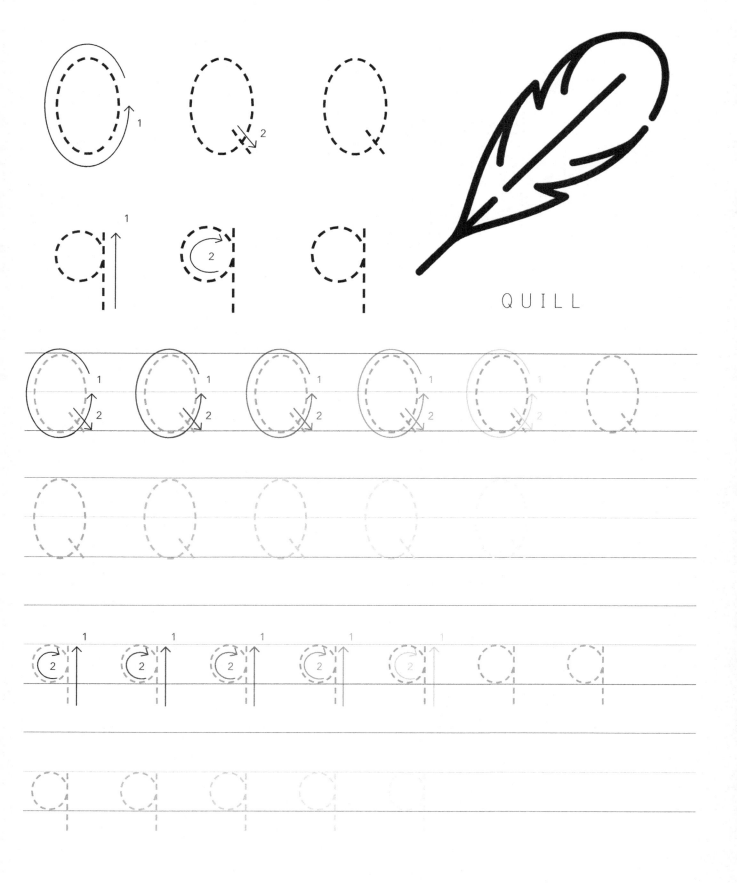

QUILL

R LIKE .....

COLOR ALL OBJECTS THAT BEGIN WITH THE LETTER R

RABBIT

S

LIKE .....

COLOR ALL OBJECTS THAT BEGIN WITH THE LETTER S

S N A K E

SSSSSSSSSSSSSS

SSSSSSSSSSSSSS

SSSSSSSSSSSSSS

SSSSSSSSSSSSSS

T

LIKE .....

COLOR ALL OBJECTS THAT BEGIN WITH THE LETTER T

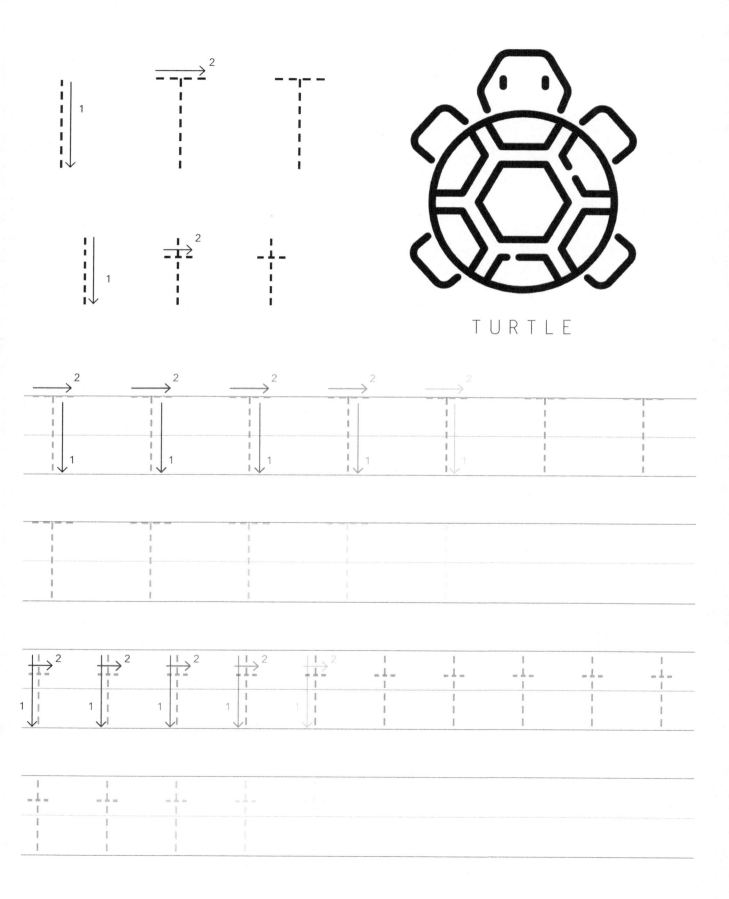

TURTLE

U

LIKE .....

COLOR ALL OBJECTS THAT BEGIN WITH THE LETTER U

U N I C O R N

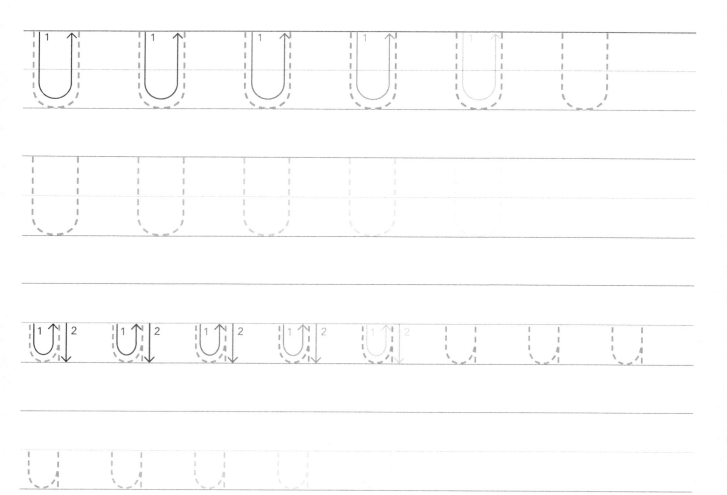

V

LIKE .....

COLOR ALL OBJECTS THAT BEGIN WITH THE LETTER V

VEGETABLES

W

LIKE .....

COLOR ALL OBJECTS THAT BEGIN WITH THE LETTER W

WATERMELON

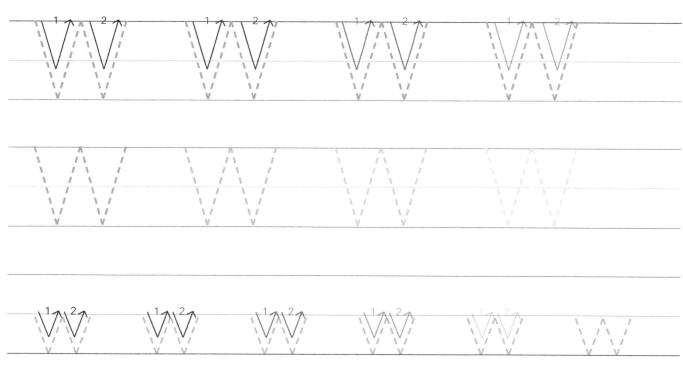

X

LIKE .....

COLOR ALL OBJECTS THAT BEGIN WITH THE LETTER X

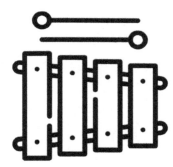

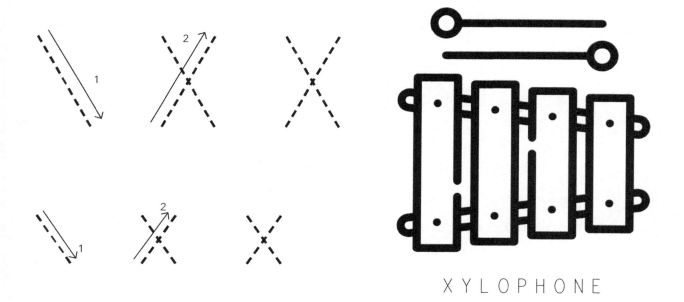

X Y L O P H O N E

Y

LIKE .....

COLOR ALL OBJECTS THAT BEGIN WITH THE LETTER Y

YETI

Z

LIKE .....

COLOR ALL OBJECTS THAT BEGIN WITH THE LETTER Z

ZEBRA

ZZZZZZZZZZZZZ

ZZZZZZZZZZZZZ

ZZZZZZZZZZZZZ

ZZZZZZZZZZZZZ

Aa Aa Aa Aa Aa Aa Aa Aa

Apple Apple

Airplane

Angel Angel

Alligator

Ambulance

Bb Bb Bb Bb

Baby Baby

Bee Bee

Banana

Boy Boy

Bell Bell Bell

Cc Cc Cc Cc

Clown Clown

Car Car Car

Candle

Camera

Cat Cat Cat

Cc Cc Cc Cc

Clown Clown

Car Car Car

Candle

Camera

Cat Cat Cat

Dd Dd Dd Dd

Dog Dog

Doctor Doctor

Donut Donut

Domino

Duck Duck

Ee Ee Ee Ee

Elephant

Egg Egg Egg

Eye Eye Eye

Education

Earth Earth

te te te te

Ff Ff Ff Ff Ff

Fish Fish Fish

Flower Flower

Flamingo

Family Family

Foot Foot Foot

Gg Gg Gg Gg

Giraffe

Guitar Guitar

Grape Grape

Grass Grass

Gold Gold

Hh Hh Hh Hh Hh

Horse Horse

Hello Hello

Hand Hand

Home Home

House House

Hh Hh Hh Hh Hh

Ii Ii Ii Ii Ii Ii Ii

Internet

Iguana Iguana

Ice cream

Island Island

Igloo Igloo

Jj Jj Jj Jj Jj

Jaguar

Juice Juice

Jelly Jelly

Jam Jam

Jacket

Kk Kk Kk Kk

Koala Koala

Kiss Kiss

King King King

Kite Kite

Kangaroo

Ll Ll Ll Ll Ll Ll Ll Ll Ll

Lamp Lamp

Love Love Love

Lamb Lamb

Lion Lion

Ladybug

Mm Mm Mm

Moon Moon

Mango Mango

Mum Mum Mum

Monkey

Mouse Mouse

Nn Nn Nn Nn

Nose Nose

Nail Nail Nail

Night Night

Nine Nine Nine

Number

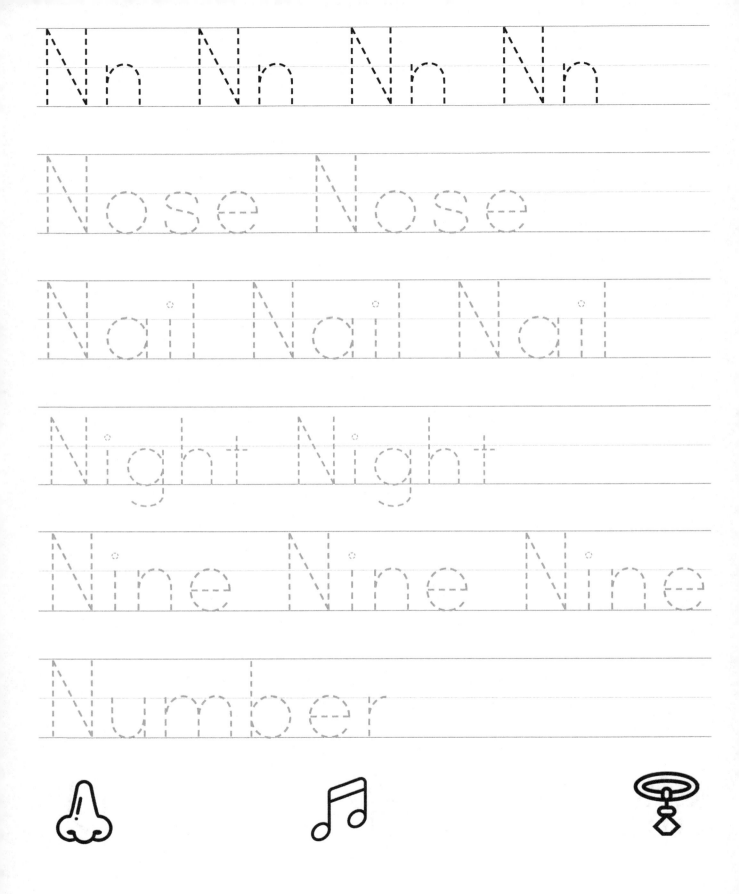

Nn Nn Nn Nn Nn

Oo Oo Oo Oo Oo Oo Oo Oo

Owl Owl Owl

Ocean Ocean

Organe

Onion Onion

Octopus

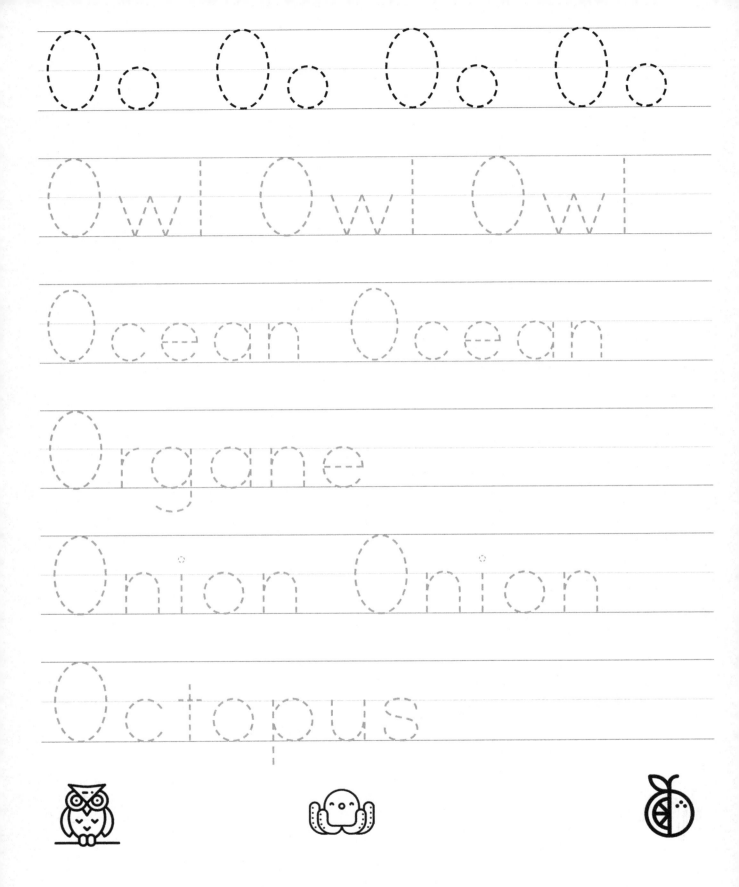

Pp Pp Pp Pp

Pizza Pizza

Pig Pig Pig Pig

Peacock

Pineapple

Penguin Penguin

Qq Qq Qq Qq

Queen Queen

Quarter

Quill Quill

Quit Quit Quit

Quack Quack

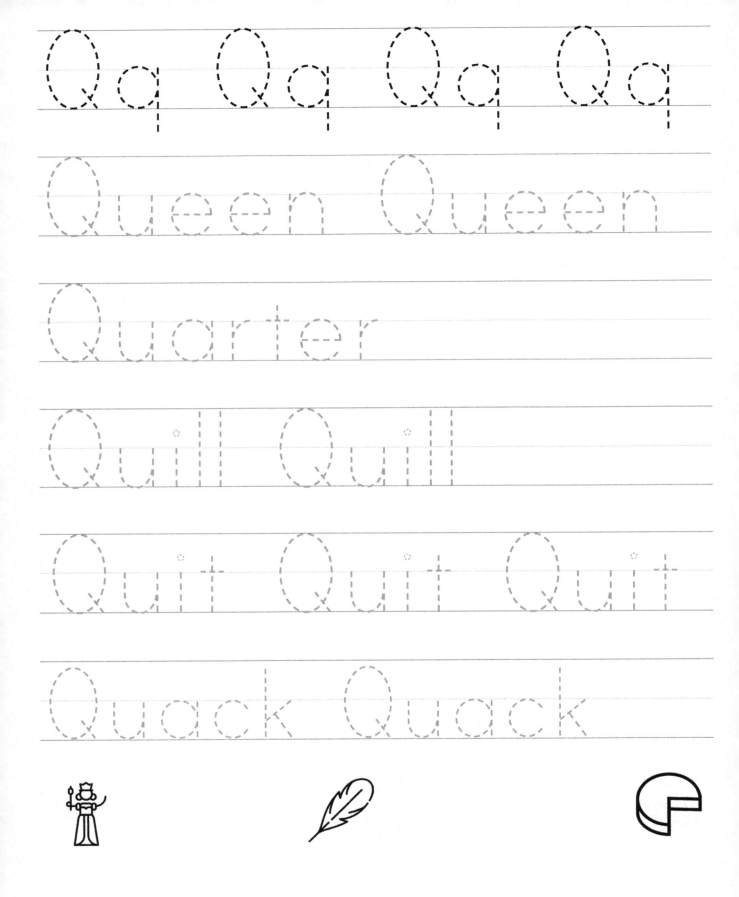

Rr Rr Rr Rr Rr

Rabbit Rabbit

Rainbow

Radio Radio

Ring Ring Ring

Rat Rat Rat

Ss Ss Ss Ss

Sun Sun Sun

Snail Snail

Stars Stars

Snake Snake

School School

Ss Ss Ss Ss

Tt Tt Tt Tt Tt

Tomato

Tiger Tiger

Turtle Turtle

Train Train Train

Tea Tea Tea

Uu Uu Uu Uu Uu

Umbrella

Ufo Ufo Ufo

Unicorn

Uncle Uncle

Ukelele Ukelele

Vv Vv Vv Vv Vv

Vampire

Vegetable

Video Video

Vase Vase

Volleyball

V V V V V V V

Ww Ww Ww

Window

Whale Whale

Wolf Wolf

Watermelon

Wheel Wheel

X x   X x   X x   X x

Xylophone

X-Ray X-Ray

Xoxo Xoxo Xoxo

Xmax Xmax

Xbox Xbox

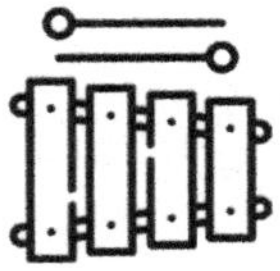

Yy Yy Yy Yy Yy

Yeti Yeti Yeti

Yogurt Yogurt

Yoga Yoga

Yacht Yacht

Yellow Yellow

Zz Zz Zz Zz Zz

Zebra Zebra

Zero Zero

Zigzag

Zucchini

Zoo Zoo Zoo

IMPRESSUM

Bei Fragen & Anregungen:
feedback@mertens-publication.de

1. Auflage

© 2018 Mertens Verlagsgruppe

Mertens Ventures Ltd.
Tinou 18, C02
7040 Oroklini
Zypern

E-Mail: kontakt@mertens-publication.de

Icon made by Freepik from www.flaticon.com
Lektorat und Korrektorat: Andrea Grube
Illustrationen: Mary Sand

Made in the
USA
Monee, IL